Original title:
Finding My Smile

Copyright © 2024 Swan Charm
All rights reserved.

Author: Kätriin Kaldaru
ISBN HARDBACK: 978-9916-89-805-5
ISBN PAPERBACK: 978-9916-89-806-2
ISBN EBOOK: 978-9916-89-807-9

Streams of Joyful Contentment

In quiet waters, blessings flow,
Hearts awaken, faith in tow.
With every breath, a gift we find,
In streams of joy, our souls aligned.

The dawn brings light, a holy grace,
Each step we take, a sacred space.
With open hearts, we seek the divine,
In tranquil depths, our spirits shine.

Sacred Songs of Elation

In harmony, the angels sing,
Of hope and love, our offering.
With raised hands, we lift our voice,
In sacred songs, our hearts rejoice.

The stars above, a choir bright,
Illuminate our path with light.
Together, we proclaim His name,
In songs of joy, we spread the flame.

Spirits in Bloom

Like flowers bright that touch the sky,
Our spirits dance, we rise up high.
In every petal, grace unfolds,
A garden rich with tales retold.

With whispered prayers, the breezes sway,
In love's embrace, we find our way.
Life's vibrant hues, a sacred trust,
In spirits bloom, we rise from dust.

The Harvest of Happiness

In fields of gold, the bounty waits,
With thankful hearts, we share our fates.
Each grain a joy, a promise made,
In harvest fields, our fears allayed.

We gather close, our spirits free,
In every smile, a jubilee.
With hands entwined, we sow the seeds,
In love's embrace, fulfilling needs.

Glimmers of Grace

In the silence of the dawn, I find,
Soft whispers of love, gentle and kind.
Each bead of dew, a promise anew,
Reflecting the hope that guides me through.

Beneath the stars, I feel a touch,
From hands unseen, yet holding so much.
In shadows deep, His light shall rise,
Illuminating hearts beneath the skies.

Through trials fierce, His strength abides,
As faith weaves paths where peace resides.
With every breath, a prayer I weave,
In glimmers of grace, I truly believe.

The Heart's Radiance

In stillness, the heart finds its song,
A melody sweet, to which we belong.
With open arms, we seek the light,
Guided by love through the darkest night.

Each moment cherished, each kindness sown,
Fosters the seeds of a love well-known.
In joyous laughter, in tears, it's clear,
The heart's radiance, forever dear.

With every heartbeat, a story grows,
Of grace and mercy, the world bestows.
In gentle whispers, truth shall thrive,
Through the heart's radiance, we come alive.

The Path to Bliss

Upon the path where shadows fade,
Each step is grace, a promise made.
With faith as guide, we journey forth,
To realms of joy, where souls find worth.

The sun breaks forth, a golden hue,
Painting the sky in colors true.
In nature's arms, we find our peace,
The path to bliss shall never cease.

With every heartbeat, love will flow,
In sacred places, spirits grow.
Eternal whispers in the breeze,
Lead us to bliss, our hearts at ease.

Celestial Revelations

In twilight's glow, the heavens speak,
A tapestry of stars, their beauty unique.
With cosmic whispers, they reveal,
The mysteries of life, so profound and real.

Through sacred sighs, the universe sings,
Of love eternal and the joy it brings.
Every heartbeat synced with the divine,
In celestial revelations, we intertwine.

Upon the winds, a truth unfolds,
A journey to be shared, a story told.
In every soul, a spark ignites,
Celestial revelations guide our sights.

Anointed with Laughter

In the quiet dawn, a whisper flies,
Joy illuminates the darkened skies.
Hearts unite in a sacred dance,
Lifted by grace, lost in a trance.

Blessed are the souls who find the light,
In laughter's arms, all fears take flight.
A melody sweet, pure and bright,
Unfolding gifts from Heaven's height.

Tears of joy flow from every eye,
As we gather, never asking why.
Together we sing, our spirits soar,
In His embrace, we seek for more.

Each chuckle a prayer, each smile divine,
In unity, our hearts align.
With arms wide open, love shall reign,
Through hills and valleys, joy unchained.

Anointed we stand, no longer alone,
In laughter's light, we have grown.
As dawn breaks forth, we rise anew,
With laughter's blessing, we walk in true.

The Majesty of Beloved Smiles

In gardens where the flowers bloom,
The fragrance of grace dispels all gloom.
A smile given, a heart set free,
Reflects the love that's meant to be.

Glistening like stars in the vast night sky,
Beloved smiles teach us to fly.
In their warmth, the world seems right,
A gentle guide through the darkest night.

With every smile, the heart ignites,
A beacon of hope in darkest nights.
In sacred gatherings, we're entwined,
With every glance, more love defined.

Let kindness flow from every lip,
In shared joy, let our faith equip.
For every smile, a blessing flows,
In the light of love, our spirit grows.

Rejoice and sing with grateful hearts,
For each beloved smile imparts.
In the tapestry of life, we weave,
The majesty of grace, we believe.

Whispers of Joyful Creation

In the stillness of the morn,
Life's beauty gently born.
Every leaf and singing bird,
A melody of love, unheard.

Mountains rise with grace adorned,
In the light of hope, reborn.
Streams of mercy flow within,
Where the heart's true song begins.

Celestial bodies dance and gleam,
Casting light on every dream.
Nature's canvas, vast and bright,
Crafts a world of pure delight.

With each breath, a prayer ascends,
As creation's joy transcends.
In the harmony, we find peace,
From endless love, our souls release.

Together in this space divine,
Hearts entwined, forever shine.
In the whispers soft and clear,
We find the joy that draws us near.

The Dawn of Inner Bliss

Awake, my soul, the sun shall rise,
With golden hues that paint the skies.
In quiet moments, feel the grace,
Of love that holds us in its space.

Chasing shadows, fears allayed,
The heart unfolds, the spirit swayed.
In solitude, the truth we find,
A gentle whisper, pure and kind.

The dawn reflects on tranquil seas,
In every wave, a hidden peace.
Breath of life, so fresh and pure,
In this stillness, we endure.

With gratitude, we walk this path,
Radiant joy, the aftermath.
Every step a hymn, a prayer,
In every heartbeat, love laid bare.

So rise anew, embrace the light,
Let inner bliss be your guiding rite.
In sacred stillness, we shall dwell,
With all creation, we weave our spell.

A Pilgrimage to Joy

We journey forth on sacred ground,
Where joy and love can both be found.
Each step we take, a song of praise,
In every heart, the light displays.

Through valleys deep and mountains high,
We seek the truth, the reason why.
With open hands and lifted hearts,
The world reflects our truest arts.

Fleeting moments, treasures rare,
In kindness shared, we learn to care.
With every face, a story told,
In laughter bright, in hands we hold.

The road may twist, the path may bend,
With faith as guide, our spirits mend.
In sacred circles, we rejoice,
In unity, we find our voice.

So let us walk, both strong and free,
In this pilgrimage, found in thee.
With every dawn, new joys we greet,
In the dance of life, our souls shall meet.

Echoes of Celestial Delight

In the night's embrace, stars awake,
Whispers of light, the heavens shake.
Each twinkle tells a tale of grace,
In cosmic dance, we find our place.

The moonlight bathes the world in peace,
As dreams and hopes begin to cease.
In silent prayer, our hearts ascend,
To realms where love shall never end.

Echoes travel through the air,
Songs of joy beyond compare.
In every heartbeat, a rhythm flows,
Connecting us to love that grows.

In the garden of the soul, we play,
Where faith and wonder lead the way.
In twilight's glow, with hearts set free,
We find the light's eternity.

So let us linger in the night,
Embrace the echoes, feel the light.
For in this space, we are complete,
In celestial delight, our lives repeat.

Beneath the Veil of Sorrow

In shadows deep our spirits wait,
Faith whispers soft, embracing fate.
With tears that fall like morning dew,
We find our strength in love so true.

The path may twist, the night be long,
Yet in our hearts, we sing a song.
For every loss, a lesson gleams,
And hope revives our shattered dreams.

As dawn breaks through the heavy gray,
The light of grace will guide our way.
With open arms, we rise anew,
Beneath the veil, we find our view.

In every trial, a gift we gain,
Our spirits free, unbound by pain.
Through sorrow's lens, we come to see,
The beauty in life's mystery.

The Sacred Breath of Happiness

In gentle whispers, joy resides,
A sacred breath that never hides.
With every smile, we touch the Divine,
In simple acts, love will shine.

The sunlit morn, a canvas bright,
Paints blessings all with pure delight.
With hearts aligned to goodness' song,
We dance through days where we belong.

In laughter's echo, grace unfolds,
With every story, life retolds.
Through moments shared, we find our place,
In unity, we share His grace.

Let kindness flow, a river wide,
In compassion's arms, we will abide.
For happiness is not a quest,
But in our love, we find our rest.

Illuminated Through Trials

In darkened valleys, faith ignites,
With every step, the spirit fights.
Through trials faced, we learn to stand,
And build our dreams upon this land.

Each challenge met becomes a guide,
To deeper truths we cannot hide.
For in the fire, the gold will gleam,
Awakening the strongest dream.

Our hearts ablaze with wisdom's spark,
In unity, we brave the dark.
Resilience blooms where courage grows,
And from the depths, the spirit flows.

With every scar, a tale is spun,
In battles fought, the victory won.
For life's mosaic, rich and vast,
Illuminates the shadows cast.

The Resurrected Heart's Lilt

From ashes rise, the heart reborn,
With melodies of hope adorn.
In whispers sweet, the spirit sings,
Of love that blooms and joy that springs.

With arms outstretched, we greet the morn,
In every dawn, new life is sworn.
For in the silence, truths take flight,
Transforming darkness into light.

A joyous dance of faith's embrace,
In every heartbeat, see His grace.
With trust renewed, we find our way,
Through every night, we greet the day.

So let the music rise and swell,
A hymn of love, a sacred spell.
For in the resurrection's art,
We find our peace, the lilt of heart.

Echoes of the Divine Heart

In quiet whispers, angels sing,
A sacred hymn, to love they bring.
With each soft breath, the spirit flies,
In grace, we find where true joy lies.

Beneath the stars, in night's embrace,
We seek the light, and find His face.
A heart that beats, with sacred fire,
Awakens dreams, lifts us higher.

In every tear, a prayer is sown,
In every smile, we're never alone.
The echoes call, from depths within,
A journey starts, where love begins.

Through trials dark, faith guides us on,
In shadows cast, He is our dawn.
With open hearts, we share the light,
Together, we transcend the night.

In unity, our voices blend,
With hopes and dreams that never end.
The divine touch, in every part,
We find our peace, the divine heart.

The Paradise of Inner Serenity

In gentle folds of morning light,
The soul awakens, pure delight.
A silent place where stillness reigns,
In harmony, the spirit gains.

Through humble paths, the heart shall tread,
In tranquil fields, by love we're led.
With every breath, a moment's grace,
In inner peace, we find our space.

The flowing stream of time so sweet,
In sacred trust, our lives complete.
With open hands, we gather love,
In quietude, we look above.

Beyond the noise, in sacred trust,
We cultivate the heart's pure lust.
A paradise where joy is found,
In every heart that beats profound.

As blossoms bloom, and seasons change,
We welcome peace, so free, so strange.
Through every trial, and every plea,
The paradise of inner serenity.

The Eternal Well of Happiness

In valleys deep, where waters flow,
An eternal well, where blessings grow.
With every drop, a joy is shared,
In clear reflections, hearts laid bare.

From tangled roots, the spirit leaps,
In sacred trust, the promise keeps.
With kindness shown, in every deed,
From simple acts, the heart is freed.

In laughter's song and love's embrace,
We see the truth within His grace.
The well runs deep, with joy to fill,
In faith's pure light, we drink our fill.

With every sip, we feel alive,
In unity, together strive.
The world transformed, when love is near,
In gratitude, we shed all fear.

Through every dawn, and twilight's kiss,
We find the joy in life's sweet bliss.
In timeless depth, our spirits soar,
The eternal well, forevermore.

A Tapestry Woven with Light

In threads of gold, our souls entwine,
A tapestry, both yours and mine.
Each color tells a sacred tale,
In beauty found, we shall not fail.

With every stitch, our hearts engage,
In laughter shared, we turn the page.
Together, weaving love's design,
In sacred art, our spirits shine.

From dark to light, the journey flows,
In every strand, the spirit knows.
With hands combined, we craft the dream,
In unity, we spark the gleam.

A canvas wide, with hues so bright,
Reflecting truth, we find our sight.
In love's embrace, we come alive,
A tapestry, where all will thrive.

Through trials faced, and joy embraced,
The weave of life, in love is laced.
In connection deep, our hearts unite,
A tapestry woven with light.

Blessings of a Happy Heart

In the morning light, we rise,
With grateful whispers to the skies,
Each heartbeat echoes, soft and clear,
A symphony of love, drawing near.

Gifts of kindness, we freely share,
Brightening the world, with gentle care.
In laughter's grace, our spirits bloom,
A tapestry woven, dispelling gloom.

In every challenge, faith will guide,
With open hearts, we walk beside.
Through trials faced, our spirits soar,
For in His love, we find our core.

With hands uplifted, we embrace,
The blessings draped in His warm grace.
Together in this joyful dance,
We find life's meaning, in every chance.

And when the evening sky fades low,
We'll gather strength from love's warm glow.
For in a happy heart, we find,
The sacred truth of the divine.

Serene Serenity

In quiet moments, peace unfolds,
A gentle spirit, calm and bold.
The world outside may roar and sway,
Yet in our hearts, stillness will stay.

Beneath the stars, the whispers hum,
Of timeless grace, allowing calm.
In nature's arms, we find our place,
Each breath a prayer, a sacred space.

With every sunrise, new hope awakes,
Serenity's song, our hearts partake.
The wind carries prayers to the skies,
In tranquil trust, our spirit lies.

With each soft raindrop, blessings flow,
A reminder of love, our hearts will know.
Through each life's season, peace shall reign,
In serene serenity, joy remains.

And as the moonlight gently glows,
We find the light in all that flows.
With faith as anchor, we drift free,
In waves of grace, we cease to be.

The Countenance of Joy

Oh, face aglow with love divine,
In every smile, the light will shine.
Each laughter shared, a sacred song,
The countenance of joy, where we belong.

In trials faced, our strength revealed,
Through every tear, our hearts are healed.
Every moment blessed, in God's embrace,
The radiance of joy, we seek and trace.

In kindred souls, compassion grows,
A circle of warmth, love's gentle flows.
As hands unite, and spirits bend,
The countenance of joy shall never end.

In service rendered, grace is found,
A joyous heart, in love profound.
Through simple acts, our spirits rise,
In gratitude, behold the skies.

So let us walk, with hearts set free,
In unity, our spirits agree.
For in our joy, we shall proclaim,
The countenance of love, a sacred flame.

A Sacred Awakening

Awake, my soul, to morning's grace,
In every moment, seek His face.
A sacred journey lies ahead,
With faith as light, we shall be led.

Each dawn a chance to start anew,
With open hearts, our spirits true.
In silence deep, His voice will call,
A sacred awakening for us all.

The whispers of the wind, we hear,
As nature sings, we draw so near.
With every step, our hearts align,
In sacred rhythms, love will shine.

Through trials faced, let courage dwell,
In every storm, we rise and swell.
With hope as anchor, we unite,
A sacred awakening brings forth light.

So let us honor the path we tread,
With humble hearts, by faith we're led.
In gratitude, let praises flow,
A sacred awakening, Love we know.

Celestial Harmony

In the realm where angels sing,
A melody of love takes wing.
Stars align in heavenly dance,
Guided by a cosmic chance.

The moonlit path of faith reveals,
A truth that every soul conceals.
Harmony in the heart of night,
A beacon of eternal light.

In gentle whispers from above,
The call to unite in pure love.
Celestial songs of joy proclaim,
The world is blessed, all are the same.

With every prayer, the spirit soars,
Unlocking heaven's ancient doors.
In unity, we find our peace,
A sacred bond that will not cease.

The Blessed Ambrosia of Cheer

In morning's light, a smile is born,
A gentle grace each heart adorns.
Sweet nectar flows, our spirits lift,
The blessed ambrosia, a precious gift.

Through trials faced and burdens shared,
Compassion blooms, for all have cared.
In every laugh, a sacred trace,
Of joy that time cannot erase.

When shadows fall and hope seems lost,
We gather close, despite the cost.
Together we rise, our voices blend,
In love's embrace, we shall transcend.

May gratitude fill each sacred space,
And guide us with its warm embrace.
In laughter's light, we find our way,
The blessed ambrosia of the day.

Wings of Tranquility

On wings of peace, our spirits glide,
In gentle silence, we abide.
The world may roar, with tumult loud,
But in our hearts, we're safe and proud.

Through every storm, we seek the calm,
A soothing balm, a whispered psalm.
With faith as our eternal guide,
In tranquil grace, we shall reside.

Beneath the heavens, vast and blue,
We find our strength, our love rings true.
In every breath, the promise flows,
A peace that only heaven knows.

With open hearts, we share the light,
In unity, we banish night.
Together we rise, our visions clear,
On wings of tranquility, we steer.

Graceful Whispers

In the stillness of the night,
Soft whispers grace the fading light.
Messages of love, they weave,
In the heart, they gently cleave.

Each word a thread of sacred art,
Stitching together every heart.
In silence shared, our souls collide,
In graceful whispers, we confide.

Amongst the stars, a promise shines,
A guiding force through life's designs.
Through trials faced and dreams embraced,
In whispered faith, we find our place.

Let grace abound in every deed,
A tender touch, a loving creed.
In every moment, pure and bright,
We rise as one, in shared delight.

Harmony in Sacred Silence

In stillness lies the whispered prayer,
A melody of grace fills the air.
Hearts aligned in a tranquil space,
Listening closely to love's embrace.

Night brings a cloak of gentle peace,
Endless worries, a sweet release.
In sacred silence, souls unite,
Beneath the stars, a guiding light.

Each breath a hymn of praise and trust,
In every moment, the heart adjusts.
Nature sings in the softest tones,
Awakening truths deep in our bones.

The world spins slow in holy calm,
Embracing the divine, a soothing balm.
Spirit dances in quietude,
In harmony found, our gratitude.

With every heartbeat, a sacred sound,
Echoes of love, where peace is found.
Together we rise, hand in hand,
In the silence, we understand.

Divine Whimsy's Embrace

In laughter's light, the spirit soars,
A playful breeze through open doors.
Divine whimsy twirls in the air,
Inviting joy with loving care.

Colors burst in a bright array,
Painting life in a vibrant way.
With childlike faith, we leap and spin,
In each small moment, we find within.

The universe plays its sweetest tune,
As stars twinkle in the joyful noon.
Hearts entwined in spontaneous dance,
In every glance, a sacred chance.

Nature giggles in the rustling leaves,
Whispering secrets that the heart believes.
In this magic, we find our place,
A divine embrace, the purest grace.

Fleeting moments of delight abound,
In love's embrace, our spirits are found.
Together we play, in wonder we stay,
In divine whimsy, our hearts will sway.

Seraphic Smiles Amongst Ashes

Amidst the ruins, hope takes flight,
Seraphic smiles pierce the night.
From ashes rise, a tale reborn,
In every heart, a fire is sworn.

Wounds may bleed, but light will shine,
In the darkest hour, the love divine.
Through trials faced, our spirits grow,
In unity found, a vibrant glow.

Angel whispers in the still of night,
Guide us gently toward the light.
Embracing all of life's cruel turns,
From every loss, a new life churns.

With every tear, a seed is sown,
In the garden of strength, love is grown.
Seraphic smiles lead the way,
Through the shadows, into the day.

Each soul a flame, shining so bright,
Lighting the path through darkest night.
In the ash, we find our wings,
In resilience, our spirit sings.

The Altar of Joyful Living

At dawn's first light, we gather here,
In gratitude, we shed our fear.
The altar stands where hearts connect,
In joyful living, we reflect.

With open arms, embrace the day,
In simple joys, we find our way.
Each moment cherished, a sacred gift,
In laughter shared, our spirits lift.

Songs of love flow through the air,
Shared blessings bloom, beyond compare.
In service given, grace returns,
With every act, our passion burns.

Together we weave a tapestry bright,
In every thread, a glimpse of light.
With hands united, we forge ahead,
On the altar of love, we are fed.

Life's sacred dance, a holy play,
In joyful rhythm, come what may.
With every heartbeat, we celebrate,
In this altar, we cultivate.

The Chisel of Hope

In the silence, hope takes form,
A chisel shaping hearts anew.
Through trials, pain, and gentle storms,
We find the strength to push on through.

With every strike, our spirits rise,
Each crack reveals the light within.
In love's embrace, no need for lies,
We trust the heart where dreams begin.

The sculptor's hand, it guides our way,
With faith that never falters, bends.
Through darkest nights and brightest day,
We walk with Him, where hope ascends.

Each moment etched with sacred grace,
A tapestry of joy and tears.
Within His depth, we find our place,
As whispers calm our deepest fears.

So let the chisel shape our souls,
As we embrace what love imparts.
In every cut, a glimpse of goals,
A vision formed within our hearts.

Celestial Blooms in Autumn's Fade

As autumn paints the world in gold,
Celestial blooms begin to fade.
Yet in their fall, a story told,
Of life, renewal, love displayed.

The winds whisper through rustling leaves,
Each petal kissed by twilight's glow.
In every ending, hope believes,
That spring will come, as rivers flow.

With eyes upturned, we seek the skies,
The stars remind us we are known.
In faith, we rise with gentle sighs,
Embracing grace that we have grown.

The branches sway, a soft ballet,
Guiding the blooms of days gone by.
In every heart, in every way,
God's canvas stretches ever high.

Though summer fades and dusk draws near,
Each moment holds a sacred space.
In winter's chill, we shall not fear,
For love will blossom, full of grace.

Embracing Grace's Gentle Touch

In morning light, where shadows play,
We seek the warmth of grace divine.
With every breath, we learn to say,
Within our hearts, His love will shine.

The gentle touch that heals our pain,
A whisper soft, a guiding light.
Through trials faced, and joy, and strain,
We find our peace in darkest night.

As rivers flow, His mercy streams,
Through every crack, His love breaks free.
In quiet hope, we build our dreams,
In His embrace, we learn to be.

The hands that cradle fragile souls,
With tender grace, they lift us high.
Through turmoil's grip, we find our roles,
As faith ignites a sacred sigh.

Embrace the grace that comes anew,
Each moment bright, with love bestowed.
In every heart, the light breaks through,
A journey blessed, a humble road.

Serenity in Faith's Embrace

In moments still, where silence dwells,
Serenity wraps around our souls.
In whispered prayers, a peace compels,
Within His light, we lose our roles.

Beneath the stars, where dreams unfold,
We find His mercy in the night.
A gentle warmth, a hand to hold,
In faith's embrace, our hearts take flight.

Through storms that rage and trials faced,
With every step, we walk in trust.
In grace, we find our lives interlaced,
A promise pure, a bond robust.

The rivers flow, a soothing song,
With every drop, a blessing flows.
In faith's embrace, we all belong,
As love and hope within us grows.

So let us rest beneath His wings,
In quietude, our spirits rise.
In every breath, the joy it brings,
Serenity beneath the skies.

Illuminated by Laughter

In the light of joy we stand,
With every chuckle, grace descends.
Heaven smiles upon our hearts,
Laughter echoes, love never ends.

From sacred ground we lift our voice,
In unity, our spirits rise.
Miracles born from a simple jest,
In His presence, our joy complies.

Every giggle, a prayer in disguise,
A gift that shines, a treasure rare.
For in the humor of the day,
God's love is found beyond compare.

The world transforms by laughter's light,
Brightening paths we ought to roam.
With grace, we share this gentle spark,
Creating here a holy home.

So let us meet in joy divine,
In laughter's arms, we feel the grace.
With every smile, our faith renewed,
Together, we embrace His face.

A Pilgrim's Cheer

With every step, a hymn we sing,
A journey blessed, no heart in fear.
For in the grace of God we tread,
Each moment claims a pilgrim's cheer.

The path ahead, though fraught with trials,
Is softened by the light of faith.
With love's embrace, we stand as one,
Together, we find our holy wraith.

Through valleys deep and mountains high,
Our spirits soar, unbound and free.
With joy in heart, we face the sky,
In faith and hope, our destiny.

The road to grace is lined with love,
In every stumble, a lesson learned.
With every prayer, our souls ignite,
To seek the light, our hearts discerned.

Hand in hand, we'll light the way,
A pilgrimage to grace and cheer.
With open hearts, we seek the day,
In unity, we draw Him near.

The Voyage of Vigor

Set sail upon the seas of light,
With vigor, we embrace the tide.
Each wave a prayer that lifts our soul,
In faith, we find our strength and guide.

Through storms that rise, we stand as one,
Our hearts remain aglow with grace.
For in His hands, our journey thrives,
No storm can dim His warm embrace.

With every horizon, new hope blooms,
A beacon shining, ever clear.
In each endeavor, love leads forth,
Together, we'll conquer every fear.

With sails unfurled, we greet the dawn,
In unity, our burdens shared.
With passion strong, our spirits soar,
In His embrace, we are prepared.

So let us voyage, hearts ablaze,
Through every wonder, every trial.
With courage drawn from depths of love,
We chart our course with faith's sweet smile.

In the Embrace of Euphoria

In the silence of His grand design,
Euphoria dances like the light.
With open arms, we lift our hearts,
To feel His presence, pure and bright.

In moments sweet, our laughter rings,
Beneath the sun, we find our way.
Guided by His gentle hand,
We breathe in joy, come what may.

With every heartbeat, love unfolds,
A tapestry of grace and peace.
In His embrace, all wounds are healed,
From sorrow's grip, we find release.

Together, we dance through fields of gold,
Where hope and faith forever play.
In euphoria's warmest glow,
We savor blessings, day by day.

So let us sing, our souls alight,
In unity, we seek the higher.
With every note, we rise above,
In His embrace, our hearts inspire.

A Journey of Joyful Resurgence

In valleys low, we find our might,
With faith as wings, we take to flight.
Each step we take, a prayer in hand,
Our spirits rise, as we make this stand.

Through shadows deep, the light will break,
With every trial, our hearts awake.
In unity, we march and sing,
Rebirth in joy, our souls take wing.

The path ahead, though steep and wide,
In love's embrace, we will abide.
With open hearts, we gather near,
For hope ignites when God is here.

From ashes born, our spirits soar,
Reviving dreams we can restore.
Each moment dear, a chance to bloom,
In grateful hearts, we banish gloom.

A journey bold, with trust we weave,
In every heart, a chance to believe.
With laughter bright, and hands held tight,
We dance anew in radiant light.

The Cup Overflowing with Radiance

With grateful hearts, we lift our praise,
In morning light, our spirits raise.
The cup of love, it overflows,
In acts of grace, this kindness grows.

In every blessing, faith unfolds,
A story shared, a truth retold.
The warmth we share, a sacred bond,
In depths of joy, we find our beyond.

When weary souls seek gentle rest,
With open arms, we are blessed.
In shadows cast, the light shall glow,
A true companion, the heart will know.

In laughter shared, and tears released,
In harmony, our spirits feast.
Each voice a note in Heaven's song,
Together in love, we all belong.

With every prayer, our hopes unite,
In grace we stand, embracing light.
The cup of life shall ever brim,
With radiant joy, our futures hymn.

The Anthem of Forgiveness

In silence deep, we seek the grace,
To mend our hearts, a warm embrace.
With every breath, we choose to heal,
Through love displayed, the wounds conceal.

Forgive the past, let burdens go,
In kindness sown, our hearts will grow.
The anthem sings of mercy's way,
In humble hearts, we find our sway.

Each whispered prayer, a gentle plea,
In forgiveness, our spirits free.
With open arms, we gather near,
In unity, we conquer fear.

A melody sweet that transcends time,
In every heart, forgiveness climbs.
With every note, a chance to start,
In harmony, we heal the heart.

Let go of pain, embrace the light,
In love's sweet cadence, we reunite.
With every song, the soul revives,
In the anthem of love, forgiveness thrives.

Dancing with Divine Light

In fields of joy, where spirits sway,
We dance with love, come what may.
With hands uplifted, hearts align,
In every step, the light shall shine.

The rhythm flows, as grace descends,
In harmony, our hearts will mend.
Each twirl a prayer, each movement free,
In sacred space, we find decree.

With laughter bright, and voices clear,
We celebrate, casting out fear.
In unity, our souls are bright,
Together, we dance with divine light.

Through trials faced, we lift our song,
In every moment, we belong.
With every beat, our spirits rise,
In love's embrace, our hearts comprise.

Let endless joy be our refrain,
In every pulse, a sacred gain.
Dancing boldly as we unite,
In the embrace of divine light.

Divine Uplift

In the light of dawn, we rise anew,
Voices of angels whispering true.
Hearts entwined in sacred grace,
In every shadow, His face we trace.

Through trials faced, our spirits soar,
Guided by love, we seek for more.
Hands uplifted, we sing as one,
In the vast embrace of the Holy Sun.

With every step on this earthly ground,
In unity, His presence is found.
The path of light, forever we tread,
In faith's embrace, our souls are fed.

In the stillness, His voice does call,
In joyous moments, we give our all.
Each tear we shed, He holds so near,
In the warmth of love, we banish fear.

Together we rise, in hymn and prayer,
No greater power can we declare.
For in our hearts, a flame burns bright,
A divine uplift, our guiding light.

The Testament of Elation

In sacred texts, our truths unfold,
Stories of love and faith retold.
Journey through valleys, mountains high,
With every heartbeat, our spirits fly.

In laughter shared, in silence profound,
In worship's embrace, we are all found.
Though storms may rage, we stand steadfast,
For His promises, forever last.

With open arms, we greet each day,
Filled with blessings, come what may.
In the beauty of grace, we find our way,
A testament of elation, here to stay.

From rivers deep to skies so wide,
In gratitude, we do abide.
Each moment cherished, a gift divine,
In faith's embrace, our hearts align.

Let joy resound, let praises rise,
In every breath, we recognize.
For in our souls, His light will shine,
The testament of love, forever benign.

The Shimmering Soul

In twilight's hush, the stars ignite,
A shimmering soul, bathed in light.
Whispers of peace float through the air,
In every heartbeat, a holy prayer.

Through trials faced, we rise above,
Each challenge met with endless love.
In the dance of life, we find our role,
United together, a shimmering soul.

In moments fleeting, we find our truth,
In the eyes of the young, in the heart of youth.
With every sunrise, hope is born,
In each new dawn, the past is worn.

With kindness sown, the world we change,
In love's embrace, we rearrange.
Every soul a spark, a radiant whole,
Together we shine, a shimmering soul.

So let us gather, in joy and grace,
Hand in hand, in this holy space.
For love's refrain will always be,
A shimmering soul, wild and free.

Joy's Reverent Dance

With every heartbeat, joy takes flight,
In reverence, we dance in light.
With open hearts, our spirits rise,
In grateful praise, we touch the skies.

The rhythm of faith, a soothing sound,
In sacred circles, we gather round.
With hands held high, we twirl and sway,
In joyous steps, we greet the day.

Through laughter shared and tears of grace,
In every moment, we find our place.
With trust in Him, we are fully free,
In joy's embrace, all souls agree.

With every note, our hearts are stirred,
In harmony, our faith is heard.
Each twirling soul, a story spun,
In joy's reverent dance, we are one.

So let the music of love resound,
In every heartbeat, joy is found.
With grateful hearts, we take our stand,
In joy's sweet dance, O Holy Land.

Altar of Laughter

In the warmth of love we gather,
Laughter dances in the air,
Joyful hearts, a sacred matter,
Echoing praises everywhere.

With each chuckle, we are lifted,
Souls entwined, a shared delight,
In this moment, spirits gifted,
Light emerging from the night.

Together, we embrace the echoes,
Laughter weaves a sacred thread,
In this space, pure joy bestows,
Hearts unite, no words misread.

Let the whispers of our chuckles,
Flourish like blossoms in bloom,
In the peace that laughter snuggles,
Find the grace that lights the room.

With each giggle, love's reflection,
In our hearts, hope finds its place,
At the altar of affection,
We release our burdens, embrace.

Manifesting Radiance

In the stillness, souls awaken,
Radiance spills from within,
Every moment, grace unshaken,
With each breath, we start again.

Hope ignites like stars in twilight,
Guiding us through shadowed skies,
Through the storms, we seek the light,
Manifesting dreams, we rise.

Every step, a path of glory,
Illuminated by our faith,
In our hearts, the sacred story,
Shining bright, in love we bathe.

As we gather, spirits gleaming,
Hands united, hearts in sync,
With each smile, our dreams redeeming,
We become what we all think.

In the power of our vision,
Radiance transforms the night,
Through our love, a divine mission,
Manifesting pure delight.

The Sanctuary of Smiles

In this sanctuary, peace abides,
Where smiles blossom like the dawn,
In our hearts, pure joy resides,
Echoing warmth as we move on.

Every glance a gift, a treasure,
In the light, we find our way,
A gentle touch, a sacred pleasure,
Guiding us through the day.

Let us share in love's reflection,
With each chuckle, spirits soar,
In the bond, our pure connection,
Opens wide the loving door.

Together, we weave a tapestry,
Of laughter, joy, and grace,
In this place, feel the ecstasy,
A smile painted on each face.

So let us gather, hearts entwined,
In this sanctuary we create,
Where every moment, love defined,
Fills our souls, no room for hate.

Heavenly Echoes

In the silence, heavenly whispers,
Guide us through the darkest night,
Echoes of love, gentle risers,
Lifting souls, igniting light.

As we walk on paths of grace,
The world softens; hearts align,
Every footstep, a sacred place,
In the echo, love's design.

Embrace the rhythm, hear the song,
Of angels leading us on high,
In this harmony, we belong,
Each note a blessing from the sky.

Let the echoes guide our dreaming,
Hearts ignited, spirits free,
In the love that keeps redeeming,
We embrace our destiny.

As we gather, voices blending,
In the chorus of the kind,
With every prayer, hope extending,
Heavenly echoes intertwined.

Hymn of Happiness

In the light of dawn's embrace,
Joy awakens every grace.
With each heart that start to sing,
Blessings flow, oh happiness brings.

From the depths of grateful hearts,
Love ignites, a spark that starts.
In the harmony we find,
Hope and peace forever bind.

In the whispers of the breeze,
Faith ignites like ancient trees.
With each step along the way,
Faithful souls in love shall stay.

Joyful voices fill the air,
In our moments, sweet and rare.
Let each smile be our song,
In togetherness, we belong.

Hearts united, strong and pure,
In the light, we shall endure.
Hymn of happiness we raise,
In this love, we sing our praise.

The Sanctity of Smiles

In a world where kindness grows,
Every smile, a gentle rose.
With each curve, a promise made,
In that warmth, all fears do fade.

Whispers soft, like morning dew,
In each laugh, an angel's cue.
Together in this sacred dance,
Hearts uplifted in each glance.

Smiles reflect the soul's delight,
Guiding us from dark to light.
With each gesture, love's embrace,
In this truth, we find our place.

Through the trials, pain may weave,
In our smiles, we still believe.
For the love we share in kin,
Brings us peace, our hearts shall win.

Joyous echoes of our past
In this moment, love will last.
The sanctity of smiles divine,
In each other, we shall shine.

Celestial Joy in Every Breath

With each breath, a gift unfolds,
Celestial joy that never holds.
In the stillness, we shall find,
Life's sweet meaning intertwined.

Every heartbeat tells the tale,
In love's arms, we will not fail.
Through the storms, we rise again,
In this journey, free from pain.

In the silence, wisdom speaks,
Hearts uplifted, spirit seeks.
With each step upon this earth,
We embrace the sacred birth.

In the laughter of the stars,
Hope resides, no door ajar.
With each moment, grace we share,
Celestial joy is everywhere.

In the dawn and twilight's glow,
In these blessings, love we know.
Celestial joy in every breath,
In life's journey, beyond death.

Sacred Whispers of Laughter

In the night, where shadows dwell,
Echoes of laughter weave a spell.
In the warmth of friendship's light,
Sacred whispers take their flight.

Joy is found in gentle jest,
In every heart, we are blessed.
With each giggle, burdens fade,
In this moment, love is laid.

As the stars above us shine,
Trust in laughter, pure and fine.
Through the trials, we believe,
In this joy, our souls perceive.

Kindred spirits, side by side,
In our laughter, we confide.
With each smile, the world we mend,
In these moments, love we send.

So let the sacred laughter ring,
In every heart, let joy take wing.
Whispers echo, bright and clear,
In this unity, we hold dear.

Elysian Laughter

In fields where angels sing and dance,
Hearts rejoice in sweet romance.
With every sound, the spirit soars,
A hymn of bliss through open doors.

The laughter flows like gentle streams,
A gift of grace within our dreams.
With every chuckle, peace will reign,
A sacred bond that will sustain.

In moments shared beneath the sky,
We gather close, we lift on high.
In joyful mirth, we praise His name,
Through laughter, love, and endless fame.

Elysian winds whisper our fate,
In joy, we gather, never late.
As echoes of our laughter blend,
In Heaven's light, our souls ascend.

With every laugh, a vow we make,
To cherish joy for heaven's sake.
In unity, we find our peace,
In laughter's grace, our souls release.

Sacred Gardens of Joy

In gardens where the lilies bloom,
Where scents of faith dispel all gloom.
Each petal whispers tales divine,
In sacred realms, our spirits shine.

The sunlight dances on the leaves,
A testament to love that breathes.
Among the blooms, we yield our hearts,
In joyful praise, the journey starts.

With hands uplifted to the skies,
We find our strength as hope complies.
In every seed, a promise thrives,
In sacred soil, our joy revives.

We walk together, hand in hand,
In gardens blessed, a holy land.
With laughter ringing, spirits soar,
In sacred joy, we seek for more.

In unity, our voices rise,
A choir blessed, we are the prize.
In sacred gardens, together we sing,
A hymn of joy, to Him we bring.

The Light of Laughter

In shadows deep, where hope seemed lost,
A spark ignites, no matter the cost.
The light of laughter breaks the night,
A guiding star, so warm and bright.

Upon our lips, a joyful song,
In laughter's arms, we all belong.
With every chuckle, spirits rise,
Reflecting grace before our eyes.

The echo of joy in every heart,
A sacred love that won't depart.
In moments shared, our burdens light,
Together, we embrace the light.

The light of laughter shines so clear,
A glimpse of Heaven, drawing near.
With every smile, a prayer we share,
In joy's embrace, we find our care.

As laughter dances on the breeze,
In unity, our spirits seize.
In every heart, a sacred flame,
In laughter's light, we praise His name.

The Promise of Joy

Through trials faced and valleys low,
A promise blooms, a sacred flow.
In every tear, a seed is sown,
The promise of joy, in hearts, is grown.

With every dawn, a new delight,
In faith, we walk towards the light.
The path of hope, so richly paved,
In joy's embrace, our souls are saved.

Together we rise, in love we stand,
A testament throughout the land.
In laughter shared, our strength is found,
The promise of joy forever crowned.

In every smile, a glimpse of grace,
A reminder of a loving embrace.
We carry forth, this joyous flame,
In every heart, we speak His name.

So let us sing, in unity bright,
The promise of joy, our guiding light.
With hearts entwined, we hail the day,
In love and laughter, we find our way.

The Joyful Pilgrimage

We walk the path in sacred light,
With every step, the heart takes flight.
Through valleys low and mountains high,
Our souls unfold beneath the sky.

In faith, we find our humble grace,
Each moment felt, we embrace the space.
The laughter shared, a joyous song,
Together, united, where we belong.

With open hearts, we greet the dawn,
In every shadow, hope is drawn.
The road is long, but spirits free,
In love's abundance, we shall see.

A journey sacred, shared by all,
In whispered prayers, we heed the call.
With hands held high, we seek the way,
Each step of faith, our debt to pay.

In unity we rise and shine,
The path is bright, our hearts align.
For every pilgrimage we make,
In gratitude, our lives awake.

Laughter Like a Prayer

In every chuckle, joy does bloom,
A blessed sound, dispelling gloom.
With open hearts and spirits light,
We dance in grace, our pure delight.

Laughter echoes through the night,
A prayer of joy, a beacon bright.
In every smile, a sacred vow,
To lift each other here and now.

With playful hearts, we gather near,
In every giggle, love draws near.
For laughter is a holy song,
In its embrace, we all belong.

Through trials faced, we share a jest,
In humor's arms, we find our rest.
Together, we find life's sweet cheer,
With laughter bright, there's naught to fear.

So let us laugh in purest prayer,
With grateful hearts, a joyful flare.
In every giggle, let us partake,
For laughter's gift, our souls awake.

The Spirit of Exuberance

With every dawn, new life unfolds,
In vibrant hues, the spirit holds.
Awake, arise, the call is clear,
Embrace the joy, it's ever near.

In nature's dance, our hearts entwine,
With every breath, a love divine.
The hills rejoice, the rivers flow,
A celebration, let it show.

With open arms, we greet the day,
In every challenge, come what may.
For joy is found, in every glance,
Life's exuberance, a holy dance.

With songs of praise that lift us high,
In unity, we'll never die.
Let laughter ring, and spirits soar,
In this communion, we explore.

So let us dance with hearts ablaze,
In gratitude, we'll sing our praise.
Together we weave the threads of grace,
In spirit's joy, we find our place.

Emissaries of Light

We walk as one, emissaries bright,
In every heartbeat, love ignites.
Through darkened paths, we spread the flame,
In unity, we call His name.

With every step, our purpose clear,
To guide the lost, to bring them near.
In kindness shown, the light we raise,
The world transformed by love's embrace.

Each smile a spark, each hand a guide,
In every heart, let hope reside.
Together we shine, a radiant crew,
For every soul, we'll see it through.

In troubled times, we stand as one,
With strength profound, our work begun.
In service true, we find our might,
As faithful stewards, emissaries of light.

So let us march on sacred ground,
In faith and love, our path is found.
For as we share, the world will see,
In every heart, His light shall be.

Pathways to Radiance

In the dawn's embrace, we seek the way,
Guided by love, we do not stray.
With hearts alight, we walk in faith,
Each step a promise, a sacred wraith.

Through trials faced, our spirits grow,
In valleys deep, the truth will flow.
By grace bestowed, we rise anew,
Together bound, we find what's true.

With hands held high, we sing His name,
Each breath a whisper, igniting flame.
In darkness' clutch, we hold the light,
For in our hearts, shines pure delight.

Angel's wings guide our errant path,
In moments of doubt, we feel His wrath.
Yet in despair, hope doesn't wane,
For love's embrace shall break each chain.

So let us walk, our mission clear,
In every heartbeat, His voice we hear.
The pathways bright, forever gleam,
In unity, we strive and dream.

The Light Within Shadows

In twilight's realm, shadows softly creep,
Yet in our hearts, the light will keep.
With every tear, the soul does shine,
The cross we bear, a sacred sign.

When fears arise and paths are lost,
We gather strength, no matter the cost.
For in the dark, the stars ignite,
Guiding our souls towards the light.

Through trials faced, we find our grace,
With every challenge, we embrace.
The flickering flame, our inner guide,
In shadows dense, we shall abide.

With love's soft whisper, pain is soothed,
In every heart, pure light is moved.
While darkness wraps like a heavy shroud,
We rise in faith, eternally proud.

So let this light within us glow,
A beacon bright, through winds that blow.
For shadows fade, and hope endures,
In light's embrace, our spirit soars.

Rebirth of the Soul's Laughter

From ashes born, the spirit flies,
A joyous heart beneath the skies.
In every laugh, a song of grace,
The soul reborn, we find our place.

With each new dawn, we rise again,
Free from the chains of earthly pain.
In blessed moments, laughter reigns,
Transforming sorrow into gains.

Within the storm, we find our peace,
In sacred union, sweet release.
For laughter echoes through the night,
A sacred gift, our hearts unite.

So dance in joy, let voices sing,
In every heart, love's radiant wing.
Through trials faced, our spirits blend,
In laughter shared, our hopes transcend.

With every giggle, spirits soar,
In light and love, forevermore.
So let us cherish, every smile,
For in laughter's grip, we walk our mile.

Grace in Gloomy Valleys

In valleys low, where shadows lie,
We seek the grace that's born of sighs.
With weary hearts, we lift our gaze,
Finding hope in the darkest days.

Through troubled streams, our spirits wade,
In faith we stand, though fears invade.
For every tear that gently flows,
Brings forth the strength that grace bestows.

In lonely nights when silence reigns,
We hear His voice, dispelling pains.
In quiet whispers, hearts align,
With grace as light, our souls entwine.

So journey forth through shadows deep,
In every promise, His love we keep.
For grace shall guide through every strife,
The tapestry of our sacred life.

In gloomy valleys, hope shall bloom,
With every step, dispelling gloom.
For in His arms, we find our way,
With grace, we greet each brand new day.

The Harmony of Gladness

In joy we gather, hearts aligned,
With grateful souls, our spirits bind.
Each note of laughter, a sacred song,
In harmony, where we all belong.

Through trials faced, we rise anew,
With faith and love, our hearts break through.
In every tear, a blessing flows,
The light of hope eternally glows.

From mountains high to valleys low,
His grace surrounds, like rivers slow.
Together we walk, in peace we trust,
With every step, in Him we must.

In communion sweet, we raise our voice,
In all we do, we shall rejoice.
For in His presence, we find our way,
In harmony of gladness, come what may.

Radiant Reflections

In stillness deep, the heart can see,
The mirrored grace in you and me.
Each thought a prayer, each breath a gift,
In sacred silence, our spirits lift.

The morning light breaks through the gray,
Caressing dreams that danced away.
In every shadow, a promise stands,
With open hearts and outstretched hands.

Beneath the stars, we seek and find,
The whispers soft, the ties that bind.
In love and kindness, we reflect His light,
In radiant moments, our souls take flight.

Through every trial, we stand as one,
With hearts ignited, our journey's begun.
In the light of truth, we rise and shine,
In radiant reflections, our spirits divine.

The Beatitude of Bliss

In every heartbeat, joy resides,
Through trials' storms, the spirit guides.
With open arms, we greet the day,
In the beatitude, we find our way.

The gentle breeze carries our prayer,
In gratitude rich, we softly share.
Each moment treasured, a divine kiss,
In the embrace of peaceful bliss.

With eyes of faith, we see the grace,
In nature's beauty, we find our place.
In every smile, in every tear,
The truth of love is ever near.

As sunbeams dance on fields of gold,
We carry stories of love untold.
In unity, we rise, we soar,
In the beatitude of bliss, forevermore.

Embraced by Light

Under the heavens, in twilight's glow,
We seek the path that love will show.
With open hearts and hands held tight,
We find our way, embraced by light.

In whispers soft, the spirit speaks,
Through valley low, through mountain peaks.
Each journey shared, a sacred bond,
In the embrace, our hearts respond.

With every sunrise, grace anew,
Like petals kissed by morning dew.
In every moment, His love ignites,
Our souls entwined, embraced by light.

In unity, we rise and sing,
With praise uplifted, our voices ring.
In the dance of life, we take our flight,
Together, forever, embraced by light.

The Revelations of a Content Heart

In stillness found, the spirit sighs,
Content within, where true joy lies.
Each breath a gift, each moment clear,
Faith whispers love, dispels all fear.

Morning light, a gentle grace,
In the heart, a sacred place.
With every beat, a truth unfolds,
The warmth of faith, a love that holds.

In trials faced, the soul can see,
A tapestry of harmony.
Amidst the storm, a calming part,
The blessings dwell in a content heart.

Eternal hope, a guiding star,
Leads us gently, near and far.
In gratitude, our voices rise,
Revealing beauty in the skies.

Through quiet times, through endless night,
The heart finds peace in love's pure light.
A testament to faith's embrace,
In every breath, we find our place.

Heavenly Melodies of Joy

From heights above, the angels sing,
Their joyous notes on breezes cling.
Hearts uplifted, spirits soar,
In melodies that evermore.

Songs of grace, serene and sweet,
Guiding souls on angel's feet.
Each note a prayer, each chord a light,
In harmony, our fears take flight.

Life's rhythms blend in sacred space,
With every pulse, we feel His grace.
The world transforms, and hearts ignite,
With heavenly sounds and pure delight.

Rejoice, rejoice! The echoes call,
For in His love, we rise, not fall.
Our spirits dance, in joyous play,
As heavenly melodies find their way.

With every beat, the joy we share,
A symphony of love laid bare.
In this embrace, our hearts collide,
In heavenly melodies, we abide.

The Rainbow of Delight

After the storm, a promise glows,
A vibrant path where hope still flows.
Colors bright, a wondrous sight,
The rainbow shines with pure delight.

Each hue a grace, a tender love,
A sign of peace from realms above.
The sunbeams dance on droplets clear,
Inviting all to draw near.

In every shade, a story told,
Of faith, of trials, of hearts so bold.
Together we rise, hand in hand,
Under the arches of this land.

A vibrant song that fills the air,
With laughter sweet, and voices fair.
The spectrum glows with life anew,
In the rainbow's arc, our love is true.

In unity, we find our might,
A tapestry woven, pure and bright.
Together we stand, our spirits light,
Beneath the glorious rainbow's sight.

Chords of Radiance

From deep within, a sound emerges,
A stirring force, the spirit surges.
In every chord, a heart's embrace,
The music flows, a sacred space.

Voices weave in harmony,
A tapestry of unity.
Beneath the stars, the echoes ring,
In every note, our praises sing.

With every strum, the soul takes flight,
Through chords of radiance, pure delight.
A symphony of grace unfolds,
In every heart, His love is told.

In stillness found, the sound we hear,
A melody that draws us near.
Through trials faced, we find the way,
With chords of radiance, we shall stay.

Together we lift our voices high,
In joy, in peace, we touch the sky.
With grateful hearts, we share the song,
In chords of radiance, we belong.

Streams of Celestial Light

In the stillness of the night,
Whispers of the stars ignite,
Guiding hearts with gentle grace,
In their glow, we find our place.

Rivers flow from heaven's throne,
Washing sins, we are not alone,
Each drop a promise, pure and bright,
Nourishing souls with sacred light.

Wisdom dances in the air,
Echoes of love everywhere,
Hear the hymn of angels sing,
In this joy, our spirits spring.

Branches bend with fruits divine,
Harvests filled with hope entwined,
In every seed, a chance to grow,
Boundless grace, forever flow.

Lift your gaze and seek the sky,
In the clouds our dreams do lie,
For in faith, the heart takes flight,
Streaming forth, celestial light.

Joyous Echoes of Faith

In the dawn of each new day,
Voices rise and gently sway,
Songs of hope, forever near,
In our hearts, we hold them dear.

Every trial, a step to grace,
Finding strength in love's embrace,
Lifted high by hands that pray,
Guided on our blessed way.

Fountains flow with grace so sweet,
Uniting souls in joyful meet,
Every heartbeat sings in tune,
Beneath the sun, beneath the moon.

Let our laughter fill the air,
Sharing burdens, showing care,
In the unity of light,
We discover pure delight.

Hope abounds in every heart,
Glimmers of love play their part,
In the echoes of our praise,
Joyous faith will always blaze.

Radiance of the Creator

With the dawn, His light appears,
Chasing shadows, calming fears,
In His warmth, our spirits soar,
Bathed in love forevermore.

Mountains bow and oceans sing,
In His presence, hope takes wing,
Every creature, great and small,
Reveals a love that binds us all.

Stars align in perfect grace,
Mirroring His tender face,
Guiding souls, both lost and found,
In His love, our hearts abound.

Let us gather in His name,
With our voices, fan the flame,
For in unity, we rise,
Radiance that never dies.

As the universe extends,
So our love, it never ends,
In the heart of every prayer,
The Creator's light is there.

The Paradigm of Praise

In the silence of the morn,
Our spirits rise, anew reborn,
Songs of glory fill the air,
In every note, a whispered prayer.

Gather round with open hearts,
Each one plays a sacred part,
Voices blend in sweet delight,
Weaving faith in purest light.

Mountains tremble at His call,
Hearts awaken, break their fall,
In the rhythm, we find grace,
A celestial, loving space.

Hands are lifted, faces bright,
In this dance of sheer delight,
Praise, a bond that never breaks,
In our joy, the whole world wakes.

Together we proclaim His name,
In our hearts, the steady flame,
The paradigm of faith we share,
Roots of love, planted in prayer.

The Vessel of Elation

In humble prayer, our hearts ascend,
To skies where boundless joys extend.
With faith, our spirits rise on high,
In love's embrace, we soar and fly.

Each moment blessed, our hands we raise,
In gratitude, we sing His praise.
A vessel pure, we carry light,
Through darkest woes, we find the bright.

In unity, our voices blend,
In fellowship, all fears we mend.
A sacred bond, our souls ignite,
In hope's embrace, we find the right.

We journey forth with hearts afire,
In every trial, our dreams inspire.
With trust in Him, our burdens fade,
In every dawn, His truth displayed.

So let us share this holy quest,
In every heart, His love expressed.
The vessel of our joy, we hold,
In kindness shared, our story told.

Serene Waters of Contentment

Beneath the skies of azure grace,
The waters run, a calm embrace.
In stillness, find the softest peace,
In tranquil depths, our worries cease.

With whispered winds and rustling leaves,
The heart, like river, gently weaves.
In every wave, a lesson pure,
The soul's delight, forever sure.

As sunlight dances on the shore,
In every heartbeat, we explore.
Each droplet sings of grace bestowed,
Where love abides, and joy has flowed.

In silence, we discover truth,
A childlike spirit, fresh as youth.
With every splash, we are reborn,
In serene waters, hope is sworn.

Together here, we seek the light,
In shared contentment, hearts take flight.
With open minds, we find our way,
In gentle waves, we humbly pray.

Through Shadows to Celestial Joy

In twilight's hush, the shadows creep,
Yet in our hearts, we fiercely keep.
A spark of hope, a guiding star,
Through trials faced, we journey far.

With every step, the path unfolds,
A sacred tale that gently holds.
In darkest night, a beacon bright,
Leads weary souls to morning light.

Through tempest's roar, we cling to grace,
In every storm, His warm embrace.
The shadows serve to teach and guide,
In trust, we walk by faith, not pride.

In every tear, a promise sown,
A deeper love we have all known.
Through shadows thick, our spirits soar,
To realms of joy, forevermore.

With every dawn, our hearts rejoice,
In unity, we find our voice.
Through trials faced, we boldly rise,
To celestial joy beneath the skies.

The Harvest of Grateful Hearts

In fields of plenty, blessings grow,
With grateful hearts, we joyfully sow.
Each seed of kindness, love we share,
In every gesture, God's light we bear.

As golden grains sway in the breeze,
We gather round, our souls at ease.
In harmony, we sing of grace,
In every moment, we find His face.

The harvest time, a sacred call,
To lift each other, one and all.
With open hands and giving hearts,
In loving kindness, true joy imparts.

Through trials faced, we find our way,
In gratitude, we humbly stay.
Each blessing shared, a circle wide,
In every heart, His love will guide.

Together, we reap what we have sown,
In every act, our love is shown.
The harvest of our grateful hearts,
In unity, our spirit starts.

The Eternal Dawn of Happiness

In sunrise's glow, hope takes flight,
Joyful souls embrace the light.
Each heartbeat sings a sacred hymn,
In the dawn, love's grace won't dim.

With every breath, blessings unfold,
Promises whispered, stories told.
Hearts united in faith's embrace,
Finding peace in a sacred space.

Through trials faced, we shall rise,
Our spirits soar toward the skies.
Everlasting light shall guide the way,
In the eternal dawn, we stay.

With gratitude, we walk the path,
Radiate joy, escape the wrath.
In the sacred bond, we are one,
Under the watch of the shining sun.

So hold dear the moments we share,
In the hush of evening's prayer.
For in each heart, happiness grows,
In the eternal dawn, love glows.

Amen to Joy

With open hearts, we raise our song,
In unity, where we belong.
Let laughter echo through the air,
Amen to joy, a treasured prayer.

In the stillness, peace resides,
In the laughter, grace abides.
We gather close, hand in hand,
In the sacredness of this land.

Through trials fierce, our spirits shine,
In the love, a grand design.
With faith as our guiding light,
Amen to joy, forever bright.

With each sunrise, hope renewed,
In every moment, kindness brewed.
Let us cherish, let us share,
The warmth of joy, a holy flare.

So let us sing with voices clear,
In every heart, may love appear.
For in joy, we find the way,
Amen to joy, come what may.

The Essence of Cheerfulness

In laughter's echo, spirits rise,
Where cheerfulness meets the skies.
With every smile, hearts are near,
The essence of joy, loud and clear.

In simple moments, beauty thrives,
In gratitude, our spirit strives.
With open arms, let love flow,
In the essence of cheer, we glow.

Through trials faced, we find our way,
With hope as light, we greet each day.
Together we stand, hand in hand,
In the essence of cheer, we understand.

As sunbeams dance on fields of gold,
Stories of love forever told.
In the hearts of all who roam,
The essence of cheer finds its home.

So let us celebrate this grace,
With cheerfulness, we find our place.
In the harmony of life's delight,
The essence of cheer, our guiding light.

The Dance of the Seraphim

In realms divine, where angels sing,
The dance of seraphim takes wing.
With radiant light, they fill the air,
In joy's embrace, free from despair.

Each twirl and glide, a sacred art,
Stirring the depths of every heart.
Their joyful steps, a heavenly trace,
In the dance of grace, we find our place.

With harmonies that soar above,
They weave the threads of peace and love.
As they encircle each soul anew,
In the dance of the seraphim, we grew.

Through trials faced, their light remains,
In whispered prayers, love sustains.
With every step, a promise bright,
The dance of seraphim, pure light.

So join the rhythm, feel the beat,
In unity, our hearts shall meet.
For in their dance, we find our call,
The dance of the seraphim for all.

The Heavenly Dawn

In the silence of morning light,
Angels whisper soft and bright,
Carrying hope on gentle wings,
To the heart, the new day brings.

A golden hue paints the sky,
Promises born as night says bye,
With each ray, a blessing flows,
In the warmth, our spirit grows.

Mountains bow to rising grace,
Nature sings in sacred space,
Clouds drift slow, in peace they glide,
In the dawn, the truth resides.

With every breath, we're awakened,
In His love, we are unshaken,
Hands raised high in pure devotion,
Finding peace in deep emotion.

So let us walk in the light,
Guided by faith, pure and bright,
For in the dawn, our souls align,
Finding solace in the divine.

Echoes of Delight

In the garden where laughter blooms,
The heart finds joy, dispelling glooms,
Every petal sings a song,
In the embrace where we belong.

Voices risen in sweet refrain,
Each note a prayer, love's gentle gain,
Heavenly echoes fill the air,
Whispered blessings, tender care.

As the stars dance in the night,
We find solace, pure delight,
In community, hearts entwined,
A tapestry of love defined.

Every smile, a sacred gift,
Lifting spirits, hearts to lift,
In each moment, grace bestowed,
Together we walk, love's abode.

So let us celebrate and share,
Finding joy in simple prayer,
For in this life, with hearts ignited,
We live in faith, forever united.

Graceful Laughter

With laughter flowing like a stream,
We find hope in the sun's warm beam,
Each chuckle is a sacred sound,
In pure joy, our souls are found.

Around the table, hands we hold,
In stories shared, love is told,
Every smile a laughter's spark,
Shining bright against the dark.

In the dance of life, we sway,
Together chasing clouds away,
With every step, our spirits rise,
A joyful hymn beneath the skies.

Graceful laughter lifts us high,
In each moment, never shy,
For in the light of love's embrace,
We find our true, unending grace.

So let us cherish every smile,
In this journey, mile by mile,
For laughter shared with those we cherish,
In God's love, we shall not perish.

The Light Within

Deep within, a flame resides,
A beacon where true peace abides,
In darkness, it forever glows,
A gift from Him who always knows.

With every heartbeat, it ignites,
A love that banishes the nights,
Guiding souls through trials faced,
In gentle warmth, we find our place.

Embracing all, both weak and strong,
In this light, we all belong,
For in each heart, a spark divine,
Uniting us in love's design.

So let it shine, this sacred spark,
Illuminating paths through dark,
With faith upheld, we find our way,
In the light, we live, we pray.

Together, let us share this light,
Guided by love, pure and bright,
For in our hearts, the truth we seek,
In His embrace, we shall not break.

The Revelation of Radiant Love

In the stillness of the night,
Whispers of grace take flight.
Hearts ablaze with sacred fire,
Love unfolds, our one desire.

Glistening in the morning dew,
Each promise, ever true.
Dancing in the light above,
We are woven with radiant love.

Gentle hands that mend the soul,
Binding every broken whole.
In shadows, faith will guide us near,
Through trials, love will persevere.

From mountains high to valleys low,
God's embrace will forever flow.
With every heartbeat, sweet and clear,
Heaven's song we long to hear.

In the tapestry of grace we dwell,
Each thread a story to tell.
United in the light so bright,
Our spirits soar, oh what a sight.

Heartstrings of Joy

Upon the dawn of each new day,
Gratitude in hearts will sway.
With every breath, a song of praise,
In wondrous light, our spirits raise.

Echoes of laughter in the air,
Joyful souls beyond compare.
In every moment, love descends,
Binding us as cherished friends.

Through trials faced and storms endured,
In faith, we find ourselves assured.
With every prayer, we sing aloud,
In gratitude, we stand so proud.

Together in this sacred dance,
Life unfolds in a sacred trance.
Hand in hand, we journey forth,
Finding joy in our true worth.

In community, we thrive, we grow,
With heartstrings intertwined, we glow.
In every heart, let joy ignite,
Shining brightly, pure and right.

The Divine Tapestry of Happiness

In the weaving of life's grand design,
Threads of love forever intertwine.
With every joy and tear we weave,
A story written, we believe.

Colors bright with laughter's grace,
Light and shadow, we embrace.
In every challenge, hope will bloom,
Creating space, dispelling gloom.

With gentle hands of faith we stitch,
Crafting moments rich and rich.
Each heartbeat echoes sacred tunes,
Underneath the watchful moons.

In every smile, a spark will glow,
A glimpse of heaven here below.
In unity, our hearts shall sing,
For happiness is what we bring.

So let us dance and lift our voice,
In faith and love, we shall rejoice.
In the tapestry, we find our place,
Embraced within divine grace.

Uplifted Souls

From the depths of trials past,
Hope arises, fierce and vast.
With open hearts and spirits free,
Uplifted souls in harmony.

The wings of faith will guide our flight,
Through darkest hours to radiant light.
In unity, we rise above,
Bound together in endless love.

Every tear, a gem of praise,
Reflecting grace in countless ways.
With every challenge, we embrace,
Uplifted by the holy grace.

In the garden of our dreams,
Joy flows like ever-sparkling streams.
As one, we stand, hand in hand,
In the embrace of God's command.

Awakened hearts, let spirits soar,
In endless love, forever more.
For in this journey, bold and whole,
We find the light that frees the soul.

The Garden of Unspoken Joy

In the quiet soil, dreams take root,
Every whisper a seed, every sigh a shoot.
Sunbeams dance upon leaves so bright,
In this sacred space, shadows yield to light.

Flowers bloom with colors divine,
Each petal a prayer, each fragrance a sign.
The breeze carries hopes, soft and clear,
In the garden of joy, love draws near.

The stillness holds secrets untold,
Stories of grace in the silence unfold.
With every heartbeat, the spirit aligns,
In the embrace of the garden, the soul inclines.

Under the arch of the twilight sky,
Celestial whispers invite hearts to fly.
In the tapestry woven with care,
Each thread of joy, a blessing to share.

Thus we gather, in wonder and peace,
Planting our dreams, never to cease.
For within this garden, unspoken and true,
Lies the promise of life, ever anew.

The Reconstruction of Sacred Laughter

In the ruins of sorrow, a chuckle resounds,
Echoing hope through the broken grounds.
Hearts that once grieved, now rise with delight,
In laughter, we find our sacred light.

With each joyful giggle, faith reconnects,
Mending the pieces, the spirit reflects.
Together we share in this sacred embrace,
As humor reveals the divine's gentle grace.

The melody of laughter, a holy song,
Binding our souls, where we belong.
In the rhythm of smiles, our burdens grow light,
As shadows dissolve, bathed in pure light.

Gleeful reminders through trials we face,
In the depths of despair, find sweet solace.
For laughter heals wounds that silence has made,
In the reconstruction, our faith is displayed.

So let us laugh freely, let spirits be free,
For joy is the balm of humanity's plea.
With hearts intertwined, together we stand,
In rebuilding our laughter, we touch the divine hand.

A Compassionate Heart's Bloom

In the garden of hearts, compassion takes flight,
With gentle hands nurtured by love's light.
Each act of kindness, a seed we plant,
In the soil of the soul, where we learn to chant.

From the depths of our beings, empathy flows,
Binding us closely, as friendship grows.
A flower of mercy in every embrace,
In the warmth of our hearts, we find our place.

Through trials and grief, we walk hand in hand,
With compassion as guide, together we stand.
For every sorrow, a smile can amend,
In unity's bloom, our spirits transcend.

Let our hearts overflow with love's gentle grace,
In the garden of compassion, we find our space.
As petals unfold, our truth shall reveal,
The beauty of tenderness, forever to heal.

So cherish the moments, let kindness reign bright,
In our compassionate hearts, we mirror the light.
For in love's great embrace, we find our way home,
As flowers of mercy, together we roam.

Whispers of Joy

In the hush of the dawn, the whispers begin,
Soft melodies flow, like a gentle spin.
Each note a reminder, of blessings bestowed,
In the whispers of joy, our spirits are sowed.

With every rustle of leaves, a secret is shared,
In the dance of the breeze, hearts are declared.
The laughter of children floats through the air,
In the symphony of life, love's song is laid bare.

As sunlight glimmers on ripples of grace,
We gather together in this sacred space.
With open hearts, we embrace the day,
In the whispers of joy, worries drift away.

So let us listen closely to life's gentle cue,
For joy speaks in moments, both fleeting and true.
In the warmth of connection, our spirits collide,
In the whispers of joy, we journey inside.

Thus we savor the blessings, celebrate each breath,
In the dance of existence, we conquer death.
For in the whispers of joy, we find what is real,
In the heart's quiet chorus, love's essence we feel.

Revelations of Exultant Spirit

In the stillness, whispers bloom,
Guiding hearts from shadow's gloom.
Raindrops glisten on the grass,
Echoing truths that ever last.

In the warmth of love bestowed,
Hope ignites on the winding road.
Each step we take, a sacred song,
In the dance of night, we belong.

Stars awaken, a heavenly choir,
Filling souls with divine fire.
Visions come in radiant glow,
As the spirit begins to flow.

Hands lifted high in joy we raise,
In reverence to the Lord, we praise.
Unity found in every heart,
From His love, we shall not part.

With each breath, we find our place,
In the beauty of His grace.
Let our voices boldly sing,
Of the wondrous, eternal spring.

A Soul Awakened to Light

In the dawn's soft embrace,
A heart stirs to a holy grace.
Whispers of love float on air,
Each moment felt, a divine care.

In the mirror, reflections shine,
A spirit reborn, tranquil, divine.
Paths once hidden, now unfold,
Stories of faith, in silence told.

Rays of joy through shadows sweep,
Awakening promises to keep.
With open arms, we rise anew,
In the warmth of love that's true.

Grateful hearts, forever blessed,
Find solace in a sacred quest.
Through trials past, we hold the key,
In light's embrace, forever free.

Let our souls entwine in song,
In His presence, we belong.
As dawn breaks, hope takes flight,
For the soul awakened to light.

The Choir of Blessed Laughter

In a garden where joy takes root,
Laughter dances, sweet and astute.
Children's giggles rise on high,
In the symphony of the sky.

Voices meld in harmonious praise,
Echoing through holy days.
With every chuckle, burdens light,
Hearts uplifted, spirits bright.

Gathered round the golden feast,
In joyful moments, love increased.
From every corner, smiles unite,
Creating echoes of delight.

In the play of sun and shade,
The laughter shared will never fade.
For in His love, we find our sound,
A choir of blessings all around.

With every note, a story told,
In melodies of warmth and gold.
The sweetest hymn, forever after,
Is the glorious gift of laughter.

Lifting Wings to the Heavens

On the horizon, where dreams arise,
Like eagles soaring, we claim the skies.
With faith as our anchor, strong and true,
We'll lift our wings, and soar anew.

Through trials and storms, we find our way,
Guided by light, come what may.
In each heartbeat, a promise flows,
In the whispers of love, our spirit grows.

From the depths of despair, we rise high,
With eyes turned to the ever-bright sky.
In grace, we sail on winds of peace,
In the arms of love, our worries cease.

Hands united, our voices strong,
In this journey, we all belong.
Together we stand, hearts entwined,
In every prayer, our souls aligned.

As the dawn spreads its golden wings,
Hope is birthed as the heart sings.
To the heavens, our souls take flight,
In the embrace of eternal light.

The Cathedral of Inner Peace

In silence, whispers of the divine,
A sanctuary in the heart's shrine.
Where prayer meets the breath of grace,
And love finds its sacred place.

Beneath the arch of tranquil skies,
The spirit blooms, and hope will rise.
Each moment cradled in gentle hands,
A holy journey that understands.

Here echoes of the past reside,
In every tear, the soul's guide.
Through trials faced with faith unyielding,
The light within becomes revealing.

Embrace the stillness, let it be,
The heart's cathedral, wild and free.
With every breath, the world unfolds,
A tapestry of stories told.

Find solace in the sacred now,
And greet the day with humble vow.
For in this space, all fears released,
The heart shall dwell, and love increased.

Roots of Happiness

Deep within the soil we stand,
Anchored by the Creator's hand.
In gratitude, our hearts take flight,
Embracing warmth of love's pure light.

The sunbeams dance on tender shoots,
Nourished by kindness, life's sweet roots.
Each laugh and smile, the rain that falls,
Makes vibrant life through nature's calls.

Together we weave through joy and pain,
In every storm, the strength remains.
For every tear is a seed that grows,
A garden rich, where happiness flows.

Invite the world with open arms,
Find solace in its various charms.
Deep in the earth, our spirits sing,
The roots of happiness take wing.

And so we cherish each new day,
Finding bliss in simple play.
With love as our foundation grand,
We flourish, hand in loving hand.

Wings of Grace

In whispers soft, the angels sing,
A promise of the joy they bring.
With wings of grace, they lift us high,
Through trials faced, we learn to fly.

The heart, a vessel, open wide,
With faith leading through every tide.
In every struggle, hope ignites,
And shadows fade in sacred lights.

As we discover our true worth,
Each moment shines with heaven's mirth.
Embrace the trials, let them teach,
The lessons only grace can reach.

Gently held by love's embrace,
We rise above in this vast space.
With gratitude, we spread our wings,
And sing the joy that freedom brings.

So let us soar on winds of peace,
In every heartbeat, love increase.
With wings of grace, we find our way,
In every dawn, a new array.

The Alchemy of Laughter

In laughter's echo, spirits meet,
Transforming sorrow into sweet.
The dance of joy, a healing song,
Where hearts rejoice, we all belong.

Each chuckle weaves a sacred thread,
Uniting souls where hope is spread.
From depths of trials, light emerges,
In every smile, the heart converges.

With every giggle, burdens cease,
Like drops of rain that bring us peace.
The alchemy of mirth unfolds,
As love's embrace forever holds.

In playful moments, life reveals,
The simple joys the spirit steals.
In shared laughter, truth ignites,
A bond of love that warms cold nights.

So let us cherish the gift we share,
Through laughter's grace, we learn to care.
For in this joy, our spirits soar,
The alchemy of love, forevermore.

Transcendent Joy in Everyday Life

In morning's light, a new dawn breaks,
The world awakens, the spirit shakes.
In simple moments, joy resides,
A sacred dance where love abides.

In every breath, the present gleams,
Life's miracles woven into dreams.
With open arms, we greet the day,
Transcending worries that fade away.

With kindness shared, the heart expands,
Together vibrant, as life commands.
In laughter found and love's embrace,
We touch the divine in every place.

As nature whispers secrets dear,
The essence of joy is always near.
In raindrops' song and winds that play,
Transcendent joy leads us astray.

So celebrate each moment bright,
In everyday life, find the light.
A symphony of love and grace,
In every heartbeat, a holy space.

The Gospel of Merriment

In realms of joy, where laughter sings,
We gather round, as the joybell rings.
With hearts united, our spirits soar,
In light of grace, we dance and adore.

The gentle breeze whispers sweetly near,
A promise of hope, a joy sincere.
In every smile, a story unfolds,
Of laughter shared, and love that holds.

With open hands, we share the feast,
In gratitude's glow, our souls released.
The sun's warm rays bless each tender heart,
As we take part in this joyful art.

Let every moment be filled with cheer,
For in each breath, the Divine is near.
In harmony's song, our spirits blend,
As the Gospel of Merriment transcends.

So cherish the laughter, embrace the light,
In the arms of joy, we find our might.
Let every soul, in unity, sing,
The Gospel of Merriment, our blessing's ring.

Spirit of the Lighthearted

In fields of grace, the lighthearted play,
A spirit of joy brightens the day.
With laughter like rivers, we flow as one,
In the warmth of love, life's battles won.

The clouds of worry drift far away,
In the warmth of faith, we choose to stay.
Each glance exchanged is a spark divine,
Illuminating paths, our hearts align.

From the depths of our souls, the music breaks,
With joyful melodies, each spirit wakes.
In every heartbeat, the echoes ring,
The Spirit of Lightheartedness takes wing.

Embrace the delight in all that's around,
In the tender moments, true love is found.
With hearts open wide, we rise and proclaim,
The Spirit of the Lighthearted ignites the flame.

So let us dance in the glow of the night,
With faith as our guide, we bask in the light.
Together we shine, in love interlace,
The Spirit of Lightheartedness, a warm embrace.

The Festival of Joy

In the Festival of Joy, we gather bright,
With songs of hope, we radiate light.
The drums of celebration echo and ring,
As our laughter resounds, our hearts take wing.

In unity, we weave a tapestry fair,
With threads of kindness, love fills the air.
Each smile shared lights the path that we tread,
In the embrace of joy, sorrows are shed.

The stars above shower blessings anew,
As we dance to the rhythm, hearts ever true.
In every step, a promise resides,
In the Festival of Joy, our spirit abides.

As the sun dips low, colors ablaze,
We give thanks for life in countless ways.
With candles aglow, we stand hand in hand,
In the Festival of Joy, together we stand.

So lift up your voice, let the chorus resound,
With hearts intertwined, love knows no bounds.
In this sacred space, let our spirits soar,
The Festival of Joy, forevermore.

Chorus of Cheerful Spirits

In the whispers of dawn, a joy takes flight,
A chorus of spirits sings into the night.
With voices that blend in harmonious sound,
In the heart of each moment, love is found.

Under skies of azure, laughter does bloom,
In the light of the sun, dispelling the gloom.
Each note we sing, a prayer sent above,
In the Chorus of Cheerful Spirits, we find love.

Through valleys of hope and mountains of grace,
We gather as one, in this sacred place.
With every heartbeat, a rhythm divine,
In the joy of each soul, our hearts intertwine.

So let us rejoice, let our spirits be free,
In the bond of our laughter, we find unity.
A celebration of life, let our praises ignite,
In the Chorus of Cheerful Spirits, pure and bright.

With every sunset, a promise anew,
In the dance of our lives, we rise and renew.
Together we cherish, together we sing,
The Chorus of Cheerful Spirits, eternal spring.

Milton Keynes UK
Ingram Content Group UK Ltd.
UKHW020038271124
451585UK00012B/913

9 789916 898062